WHERE RAT SNAKES FIT

HOW TO DEFINE A RAT SNAKE?

Rat snakes are a loose group of snakes, usually put in the genus *Elaphe*, that include many of the most popular pet snakes kept in the terrarium hobby. Included among their ranks are the Corn Snake, *Elaphe guttata*, with its multitude of colors and patterns produced by selective breeding by dedicated hobbyists and com- mercial breeders, and a diverse listing of other species from around the Northern Hemisphere. The American Rat Snake, *Elaphe obsoleta*, also is bred in several color varieties, while recently some of the Asian species of the genus have become prominent in the hobby.

Many rat snake species have proved to be hardy terrarium animals, easy to feed and breed, and they have become very available as rather low-cost captive-bred pets that can be found in any pet shop that stocks snakes. Admittedly most of the rat snakes in the hobby are Corn Snakes, probably the single most popular terrarium snake, but some of the other species are gaining in popularity and some day may pass the Corn in availability. Because the Corn Snake is treated in a separate volume of this series, I'll just mention it later when we discuss the American rat snakes, saving our pages for some of the species that are talked about less commonly.

There are some 39 species of snakes commonly called rat snakes, belonging to at least four major groups called genera. Typical rat snakes from both Eurasia and North America are in the genus *Elaphe*, while the

W. P. MARA

No, this rat racer, *Spalerosophis diadema*, is not a rat snake. Superficial appearances can be decieving.

Trans-Pecos Rat and the Baja California Rat are North American species placed in the quite distinct genus *Bogertophis*. Two "green" snakes, one from America (*Senticolis*) and the other from Asia (*Gonyosoma*) also are considered by most hobbyists to be rat snakes, though scientists have their doubts, especially about *Gonyosoma*.

As a general rule, rat snakes are typical colubrid snakes. They have nine regularly placed scales on top of the head, with little or no fusion of the scales. The teeth are not modified as fangs or separated into distinct groups, though in some species the front teeth may be distinctly longer than the back teeth or vice versa. The scales of the body typically have a distinct keel through the center, at least on the rows near the midline of the back. Often the ventral scales (those covering the belly) are sharply angled at either side, an adaptation to make climbing of trees easier; this gives the body a distinctive "breadloaf" shape. The tail is not especially long, with some exceptions, and the head is

organ. All rat snakes but one lay eggs, but a few species from the harshest climates of Asia hold the eggs in their bodies until just a few days before hatching and can have short incubation periods. The average hobbyist really can recognize a rat snake only by looking at the name and seeing if it is on the list, because there is no one feature that will

G. PISANI

The Green Rat Snake, *Senticolis triaspis*, is an example of a rat snake that no longer is placed in the genus *Elaphe*. Expect more changes in generic names of the rat snakes as research by herpetologists continues.

moderately distinct from the neck. As a rule, these are heavy-bodied snakes, never slender like the racers, and not especially nervous, though some are vicious biters. Many differences among the species exist in details of the skeleton of the head and the backbone, and there are a great number of differences in the hemipenes, the male copulatory

identify *Elaphe* and the other rat snake genera.

To a scientist interested in relationships among the various snakes, rat snakes are a poorly defined group. In fact, many herpetologists would say that the term "rat snake" and the genus *Elaphe* cannot be defined. Recent work places the North American rat and corn snakes and at least some of the Eurasian species in a group that is very closely related to the pine and gopher snakes (*Pituophis*) of North America and Mexico. In fact, some lines of evidence seem to show that the Pine Snake (*Pituophis melanoleucus*) is more closely related to the American Rat Snake (*E. obsoleta*) than is the Corn Snake, and

HYBRIDS

All these genera are put into a tribe, the Lampropeltini, of the subfamily Colubrinae, family Colubridae. They seem to be very closely related and have been around for at least 20 million years as species similar to those living today. Even today the various species and subspecies are similar enough that

The Jungle Corn is a striking hybrid between snakes of two different genera, a Corn Snake, *Elaphe guttata guttata*, and a California Kingsnake, *Lampropeltis getula californiae*. Don't be too misled by names, however, as many scientists feel these species are closely related, more so than you would expect from their being in different genera.

certainly more closely related than is the Nightsnake (*E. flavirufa*) of Mexico. In addition, both *Elaphe* and *Pituophis* are closely related to the kingsnakes in the broad sense (*Lampropeltis*, including the Mexican kingsnakes and the milksnakes) and to the small group of snakes derived from kingsnakes or their ancestors (*Cemophora*, etc.).

many of them can share genes and interbreed with man's help, producing a variety of hybrids in captivity, some of which have been bred and sold or have served as foundation stock for some interesting color varieties. In captivity, breeders have been able to break down the barriers of behavior and timing of breeding that prevent species from mating together in nature. Not only has it been possible to artificially produce hybrids between rat snake species in the herp room, but hybrids between several species of the major genera of the Lampropeltini also have been produced. According to breeders, *Pituophis melanoleucus, P. sayi, Lampropeltis getula,* and *L. triangulum* have been successfully hybridized with *Elaphe guttata* and/ or *E. obsoleta.* By now it is likely that other intergeneric (between genera) hybrids have been produced in at least small numbers.

Whether hybrids are a positive or negative addition to the keeping of rat snakes is arguable, but they are here and probably will continue to be bred in the future. Such forms as the Jungle Corn (a cross between the Corn Snake, *Elaphe guttata guttata,* and the California Kingsnake, *Lampropeltis getula californiae*) are beautiful animals that are often seen at specialty herp meetings, and some of the hybrids between Yellow Rat Snakes (*Elaphe obsoleta quadrivittata*) and Bullsnakes (*Pituophis sayi*) are attractive and interesting specimens.

The problem with intergeneric hybrids is that no one yet can tell what will happen when the hybrids are bred with each other or with their ancestors. Probably the hybrids will prove to be sterile or at least will be unable to produce offspring that will survive to successfully breed. At least this is what normally happens in other animal groups where intergeneric hybrids are produced through man's intervention. If the hybrids can successfully reproduce, however, they could contaminate the lineages of their ancestors when bred back to them, causing all types of

potential problems in the future. Any hobbyist dealing with hybrids and breeding rat snakes is urged to be very careful with these snakes and keep records of all breeding that may occur.

Less common than hybrids of rat snakes and kingsnakes are hybrids of rat snakes and bullsnakes. This specimen is the result of a cross between *Elaphe guttata* and *Pituophis sayi,* but it would only attract the attention of a specialist. Photo: W. P. Mara.

SPECIES

Though there are taxonomic problems with several of the species, 39 species of snakes generally are thought of as rat snakes. We won't have room to discuss all of them in this little book, but they all are discussed in my other rat snake book (with Ray Staszko), *Rat Snakes: A Hobbyist's Guide to* Elaphe *and Kin,* also published by T.F.H. This book is highly recommended for any hobbyist who is interested in more than just keeping a rat snake or two and wants to try a variety of species.

The following listing of rat snake species and their common names should help the beginning hobbyist place the names they see in the pet shops and on dealer lists. Subspecies are not mentioned here though many are discussed in Staszko and Walls.

AMERICAN RAT SNAKES
•*Elaphe bairdi*, Baird's Rat Snake
•*Elaphe flavirufa*, Nightsnake (Mexican Corn Snake)
•*Elaphe guttata*, Corn Snake
•*Elaphe obsoleta*, American Rat Snake
•*Elaphe vulpina*, Fox Snake

EURASIAN RAT SNAKES
•*Elaphe bimaculata*, Twin-spotted Rat Snake
•*Elaphe cantoris*, Eastern Trinket Snake
•*Elaphe carinata*, Stinking Goddess (King Rat Snake)
•*Elaphe climacophora*, Japanese (Kunisir Island) Rat Snake
•*Elaphe conspicillata*, Red Japanese Rat Snake
•*Elaphe davidi*, Pere David's Rat Snake
•*Elaphe dione*, Steppes (Dione's) Rat Snake

•*Elaphe erythrura*, Reddish (Philippine) Rat Snake
•*Elaphe flavolineata*, Black Copper (Yellow-striped) Rat Snake
•*Elaphe frenata*, Assam Green Trinket Snake

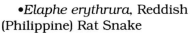

Some very beautiful hybrids, such as this cross of (supposedly) a Gray-banded Kingsnake, *Lampropeltis alterna*, and a Corn Snake, *Elaphe guttata guttata*, are truly striking. Caution is advised when purchasing or trying to breed hybrids, however.

•*Elaphe helena*, Common Trinket Snake
•*Elaphe hodgsoni*, Himalayan Trinket Snake
•*Elaphe hohenackeri*, Transcaucasian Rat Snake
•*Elaphe japonica*, Northern Japanese Rat Snake
•*Elaphe leonardi*, Burmese Rat Snake
•*Elaphe longissima*, Aesculapian Rat Snake
•*Elaphe mandarina*, Mandarin (Jade) Rat Snake
•*Elaphe moellendorffi*, Red-headed Rat Snake
•*Elaphe perlacea*, Szechwan Rat

Snake
*   *Elaphe porphyracea*, Black-banded Trinket Snake
*   *Elaphe prasina*, Green Trinket Snake
*   *Elaphe quadrivirgata*, Japanese Four-lined Rat Snake
*   *Elaphe quatuorlineata*, Four-lined Rat Snake
*   *Elaphe radiata*, Radiated Rat Snake (Copperhead Racer)
*   *Elaphe rufodorsata*, Chinese Gartersnake
*   *Elaphe scalaris*, Ladder Rat Snake
*   *Elaphe schrencki*, Amur (Russian) Rat Snake
*   *Elaphe situla*, Leopard Rat Snake
*   *Elaphe subradiata*, Sunda (Timor)

Rat Snake
*   *Elaphe taeniura*, Stripe-tailed Rat Snake (Taiwan Beauty Snake)

THE OTHER GENERA
*   *Bogertophis rosaliae*, Baja California Rat Snake
*   *Bogertophis subocularis*, Trans-Pecos Rat Snake
*   *Gonyosoma oxycephalum*, Red-tailed (Mangrove, Green) Rat Snake
*   *Senticolis triaspis*, Green Rat Snake

SOME NON-RAT SNAKES
If you are familiar with some of the other books and articles on rat snakes, you might notice that some

P. H. BRIGGS, COURTESY OF L. LEMKE

Few Asian rat snakes enter the hobby market. Even widely distributed and abundant snakes such as the Common Trinket Snake, *Elaphe helena*, remain almost unknown to the average hobbyist. Rat snakes represent a great untapped reservoir of snakes almost unknown in the hobby.

R. T. ZAPPALORTI

The Asian chicken snakes, *Ptyas*, are interesting pets if you like very large snakes that are as nervous as the racers. *Ptyas korros*, shown here, is a relative of the racers, not the rat snakes.

"rat snakes" are not on this list and are not covered further in this book. These are snakes belonging to the genera *Spalerosophis* (rat racers), *Ptyas* (Asian chicken snakes), and *Spilotes* (tropical chicken snakes), all of which appear in the hobby on occasion. Rat racers imported from the Middle East are actually fairly common, though hard to identify to species. They are famous for the large size of their eggs, which they lay readily in captivity. *Ptyas* species from southern Asia and India are seldom seen on the American market, where *Spilotes* from tropical America are fairly common. Tropical chicken snakes sometimes are very colorful, bright yellow and black.

These snakes are not related to *Elaphe* and do not belong to the tribe Lampropeltini. Instead, they seem to be related to the racers, *Coluber* and allies (tribe Colubrini), and like them tend to be nervous snakes. All feed on mammals and birds and lay eggs. Rat racers tend to prefer dry, warm terraria (most come from deserts or dry savannahs), while *Spilotes* and *Ptyas* can be kept much like Corn Snakes and American Rat Snakes, though they like it a bit warmer. The chicken snakes can be very large snakes, with records of over 9 feet in the literature for both genera.

In the next few pages I'll try to give you enough information to keep a typical rat snake and try your hand at breeding a pair. Most rat snakes have similar life histories and keeping requirements, and the ones that are available as captive-bred specimens are easy to maintain and keep healthy. There are good reasons why these attractive snakes are among the most popular reptile pets!

KEEPING AND FEEDING

SELECTION

If at all possible, your first rat snake should be a captive-bred specimen of one of the common species. Captive-breds tend to be healthier than wild-taken animals and are not likely to need veterinary care for parasites such as intestinal worms and ticks. They usually are calmer than wild-caughts and used to handling, since they have smelled human hands since hatching. If you want a special color pattern, you have to get a captive-bred, since color variants are major rarities in wild rat snake populations.

The snake you purchase might be just a few weeks old and probably will be less than two years old. Most rat snakes mature at an age of about two to three years, and breeders try to "turn over" their stock as soon as possible, keeping only selected adults for breeding. The younger they can sell a snake, the less overhead in the way of food that they have to pay. Thus a young snake costs less than an older snake. As long as the snake has taken at least a couple of meals before you purchase it, it should adapt well and continue to feed after you take it home.

Wild-caught rat snakes may be nervous and most resent handling of any type. Large specimens can be vicious biters, inflicting deep, bloody gashes that will require alcohol, some iodine, and perhaps a small adhesive bandage or two, but will

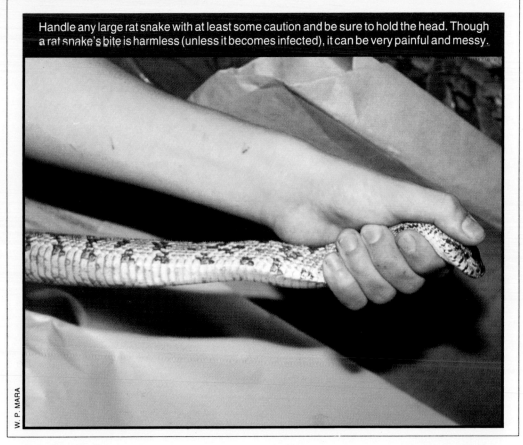

Handle any large rat snake with at least some caution and be sure to hold the head. Though a rat snake's bite is harmless (unless it becomes infected), it can be very painful and messy.

W. P. MARA

W. B. ALLEN, JR.

This Texas Rat Snake, *Elaphe obsoleta lindheimeri*, feels secure in a length of heavy PVC pipe offered as a hidebox in its cage. The pipe also can be used to hold the snake temporarily during cage cleaning if you cap it with a snake bag. A good hidebox should be dark and snug.

have no lasting effects. Even some captive-breds may be biters, but such specimens usually get used to being handled within a few days. When handling a rat snake, especially one over 18 inches or so long, be sure to use the usual grip behind the head with one hand while supporting the body with the other hand—just in case. Also, never put a rat snake, no matter how tame, next to your face, a good rule to remember when handling *any* snake.

Oh yes—make sure you have the terrarium ready *before* you buy your pet. Cardboard boxes and gallon jars are not suitable containers for rat snakes, even for a few days.

TERRARIA

For starters, the usual all-glass terrarium from your local pet shop will do well as a home for your new pet. They are relatively cheap to purchase either new or "slightly used"; are light in weight but tough; are available in a variety of sizes; and are sized to fit many different styles of lids and lights. Start with a 20-gallon terrarium. This is large enough to house most adult rat snakes yet fits well on tables and countertops without requiring special tank furniture. Rat snakes are rather sedentary, as are most snakes, and really don't need a cage much longer than their length.

Cages especially made for snakes and other herps also are excellent terraria, but they often are somewhat expensive and may be hard to find locally. Most have sliding glass or plexiglass front panels that allow easy access to the snake but may make escapes easier if the keeper is not used to handling rat snakes. Accessories may be hard to purchase locally, and often they require odd racks or other furniture to make them stable. If you plan on eventually keeping large numbers of rat snakes, special cages may be a good investment in the long run, but they are not necessary for the one-pair keeper.

Recently sweater boxes, large flat boxes of sturdy, inert plastic with close-fitting lids, have proved to be very useful for housing snakes. They are inexpensive, easy to purchase (many pet shops now handle them, often with vented lids already in place), and many can be set up in a small space using shelves or racks purchased or built for the purpose. The lids must be vented by drilling small holes through them and then securely covering the holes with fine gauze. Usually one heater and one set of lights will suffice for several boxes. The major problem is being sure that the snakes are allowed to bask and have access to full-spectrum lighting, both of which can be problems.

SUBSTRATE AND DECORATIONS

The best substrate for a rat snake, especially a small one, is plain absorbent paper, preferably unprinted newsprint. Paper is easy to replace, clean, cheap, and does a good job holding snake wastes. Unfortunately, it is not very attractive, so generally it is used mostly in hospital cages or quarantine cages in larger collections.

Rat snakes will accept a variety of standard substrates, ranging from fine smooth sand (some keepers warn of problems during molting, but if you observe your pet you should have no problems), rounded gravel (never sharp gravel), corncob mulch, and hardwood shavings, to peat moss. All work well for some keepers, and all are considered poor choices by other keepers. What this means is that you may have to experiment a bit to find a substrate that your pet tolerates well and you find easy to clean and keep sanitary. You never want a wet substrate when keeping a rat snake as blister disease (due to a variety of bacterial infections) will result.

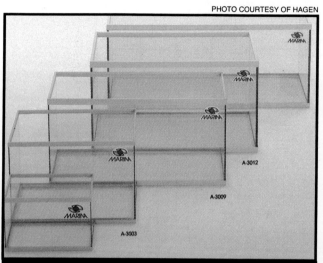

PHOTO COURTESY OF HAGEN

The best cage for a small or medium rat snake still is a good all-glass aquarium. This type of cage is durable, light, easy to find, and inexpensive, plus it is easy to purchase accessories that fit.

Provide a substrate that is non-abrasive to the snake, shows the wastes well so you can remove feces readily, and can be replaced or sterilized regularly.

A water bowl is a must with rat snakes, as they drink well from bowls. The bowl should be large enough for the snake to curl up in on occasion (but never let a snake bathe too often—remember the blister disease) yet shallow enough that drowning is not a possibility. Most rat snakes swim very well, but hatchlings may have problems. Change the water daily and never let feces accumulate in it.

Rat snakes need hiding places to feel comfortable. They do not burrow but like to wedge in under slabs of bark or pieces of ceramic flowerpots. In addition to several flattish hiding places scattered about the cage, your snake needs a hidebox, preferably one placed in the coolest corner of the cage. Your pet shop sells many different types of hideboxes sized to fit any rat snake. Remember that snakes like to have their body contact the sides of the hidebox, so do not be "generous" and buy one that is too large. The decorations also serve to aid molting.

Sturdy climbing branches of

appropriate size are not a bad idea, as many rat snakes like to climb, and some are almost arboreal (tree-dwelling) in nature. Be sure the branches are well-anchored, smooth enough not to house mites, easily sterilized, and don't come within half the snake's length from the lid of the cage.

Living plants are a waste in the rat snake terrarium, though a few nice plastic plants are not harmful. Rat snakes do not appreciate plants, living plants are hard to maintain in the heat and light of a terrarium, and the movements of a large rat snake tend to demolish any plants that come in their way. Keep the cage simple and easy to clean and you'll have fewer problems.

PHOTO COURTESY ENERGY SAVERS

Rat snakes like to bask, so they need a good basking light over their rock or branch. Be sure you buy a lamp especially made to suit your snake's needs.

LIDS

The rat snake terrarium must have a secure lid or hood, preferably one that can be attached by clips or even a padlock. Even a small rat snake is extremely powerful for its size and can force the edge of any unanchored lid that it can reach with its head. The lid must be ventilated so there is some air flow. Gauze works better than glass, which both makes the cage too humid and prevents full access to ultraviolet light by the snake. Of course the snake must not be able to reach the lid to begin with, or it will rub its snout raw against the gauze in its efforts to lift the lid. If your lights are on the lid, make sure the snake cannot get close enough to be burned.

LIGHTS

You need at least one full-spectrum reptile light, usually a fluorescent, for your snake. Most keepers recommend a day length of at least eight hours, increasing to 12 hours in midsummer. Your pet shop has a tremendous variety of suitable lights and fixtures to match them. Just make sure the light you get is made for reptiles, not

Proper heating is essential for all rat snakes, especially babies of some of the more delicate color forms. This albino Texas Rat (*Elaphe obsoleta lindheimeri*) hatchling also shows a few leucistic traits.

Never neglect to purchase a close-fitting, secure, preferably ventilated lid for the rat snake terrarium. Rat snakes are amazingly strong for their size and climb well, so take no chances.

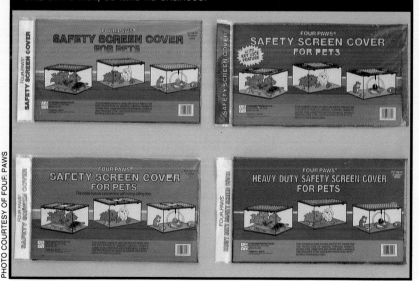

hamsters, blacklight posters, or sunbathing.

A basking light situated over a flat rock is a wise idea. Traditionally keepers have used a 40-watt incandescent bulb in a conical reflector as the basking light, but recently more sophisticated basking lights have become available, including "dark lights" that emit only

terraria. Again, put the heater as far away from the hidebox as possible.

Hot rock mechanisms consisting of a heating coil embedded in a plaster or ceramic artificial rock may be used with rat snakes if you like. They are not replacements for a basking area, however, as a snake monitors its internal temperature by judging how much heat it has received from

Many rat snakes will bask on a hot rock heater if one is provided. Together with a basking light, this may be all the heat the rat snake terrarium needs during most of the year.

heat without visible light. The basking rock and light should be placed in the corner away from the hidebox to help in creating a proper temperature gradient in the tank. The basking area need not be especially warm, 90°F (32°C) being fine for almost all species.

HEATING

Rat snakes, with a few exceptions, do well at between 75 and 80°F (24 to 27°C) during the day, dropping by about five to ten degrees at night. Species from dry habitats such as savannahs and the edges of deserts may require a bit higher temperatures, but seldom exceeding 86°F (30°C). A thermometer in or on the tank helps assure you are maintaining the proper temperature. Your lights will provide some heat, as will the basking area, but it is safest to provide an undertank heating pad or a similar heater made for reptile

above, not from below. In unusual circumstances a rat snake may literally bake from below on a hot rock without its "safety circuits" cutting in to tell it it's time to head for a cooler area. Caution is advised.

FEEDING

Rat snakes are easy to house and also easy to feed. At least captive-bred specimens are easy, because they will take pinkie and fuzzy mice. Most rat snakes take their first meal soon after they first shed their skin, usually about a week after hatching. From that point on baby rat snakes should take a pinkie (a mouse only a day or so old, with the eyes still closed and no trace of hair) or perhaps two about every two or three days. As they grow they take somewhat larger mice, first fuzzies (young mice that are mobile to some extent but still have the eyes shut and have a first coat of fine hair) and

Undertank heating pads help keep the terrarium a few degrees above room temperature and are excellent for use with baby rat snakes. Photo courtesy of Zoo Med.

You can't do without a good thermometer on your terrarium. The adhesive liquid crystal type is especially popular today.

PHOTO COURTESY OF HAGEN

then plain young mice. Adult rat snakes may take small rats as well. Large rat snakes of course may take several mice at one meal. Adult rat snakes should be fed once a week unless they appear hungry sooner; beware of overfeeding. Almost any captive-bred rat snakes can be taught to take frozen and then fully thawed mice; it should not be necessary to feed living food to a good pet rat snake. Thawing often is accomplished by taking a frozen pinkie and putting it in a cup of hot water until the body is warmed through and through.

If a hatchling at first will not take frozen, thawed pinkies, you may have to "brain" a specimen (cutting a hole through the skull cap of the mouse to expose the brains, which must have an especially interesting smell) or feed pieces of bloody mouse tail for the first few meals. Such complications are the reason many hobbyists prefer to purchase somewhat older rat snakes that are known feeders on frozen mice.

In nature rat snakes usually feed on mammals and birds, but a few species take lizards and even other snakes as a regular diet. Such reptile-eaters usually make poor pets and are difficult to maintain because food is hard to obtain on demand and it is hard to justify feeding one wild-caught reptile to another reptile. Few keepers, by the way, bother feeding chicks to rat snakes, but if you can get them easily (nutritionally best when only a day or so out of the egg) and cheaply, they can be treated much like mice, frozen and thawed.

SUPPLEMENTS

All rat snakes need regular vitamin supplements and they also can utilize calcium supplements. Young, growing specimens should have their pinkies dusted with a high-quality reptile vitamin and calcium supplement at each meal, and they must have access to full-spectrum lighting in order to properly use the supplements. As they grow older the calcium supplements can be cut back to every other meal, but the vitamins remain essential. If you are planning on breeding a female, remember that producing egg shells puts a considerable drain on the calcium levels in her body, so supplements are again essential. A female will pull calcium (and phosphorus) from the bones of her skeleton in order to provide the necessary ingredients for the egg shells. Always use supplements that are designed for reptiles, never for mammals. *No exceptions*, even if hamster and gerbil vitamins might be a bit cheaper.

So there you have it. This general outline of terrarium care will suffice for rat snakes that come from temperate climes and not especially extreme conditions. By modifying the temperature a bit it will work for both

PHOTO COURTESY OF TETRA/SECOND NATURE

A large rat snake will demolish most living plants but won't destroy a good plastic plant. If you must have plants, use plastic ones.

Many hobhyists like colorful backdrops behind the terrarium. They not only look good to the human eye but provide added privacy for the snakes.

PHOTO COURTESY OF CREATIVE SURPRIZES

R. T. ZAPPALORTI

When I was a kid in Louisiana, *Elaphe obsoleta* was always called a chicken snake, never a rat snake. They were famous for invading hen houses and eating both eggs and chicks if not detected. The American Rat Snake in all its subspecies is a good climber and will not hesitate to attack small birds on nest. Some rat snakes even have special adaptations of the backbone that help them crush egg shells.

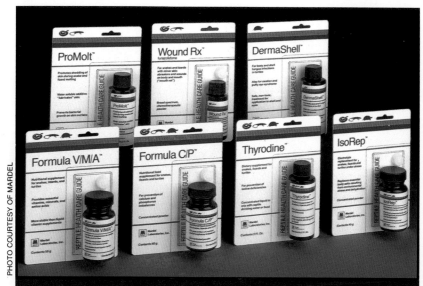

PHOTO COURTESY OF MARDEL

Though you need the help of a veterinarian for major problems, your pet shop can supply many supplements and treatments for minor accidents and ills.

the tropical Asian species and the species from the American deserts as well. The common rat snakes have not proved to be especially delicate in relation to humidity and lighting, definite advantages for the beginning snake keeper. If you purchase a captive-bred specimen about two to six months of age, you can look forward to at least ten years of successful rat snake keeping. You've made a great choice!

All the common rat snakes can be trained to take frozen and thawed pinkie or fuzzy mice available from your pet shop. Just be sure the food is *completely* thawed before it is offered to the snake.

W. B. ALLEN, JR.

The moment of truth! If you bought good captive-bred stock of a common rat snake species, kept them healthy, overwintered them properly, and then incubated the eggs under the correct conditions, you should be able to produce clutches of healthy young rat snakes like these hatching Corn Snakes, *Elaphe guttata guttata*.

BASIC BREEDING

SEXES

Before you even contemplate breeding rat snakes, you have to be able to sex them. Usually this is not a great problem if you have adult specimens. As a rule, male rat snakes have longer, more slender tails that taper gradually from a wide base. Females have shorter tails that taper more abruptly from a relatively narrower base. If you have a male and female of the same species (and subspecies where appropriate), it should be easy to tell adults apart with just a casual inspection.

Male snakes have a copulatory organ, the penis, that is deeply split down the middle so it looks like two separate organs, the hemipenes. The hemipenes are hollow sacs covered with various spines and papillae and having a groove along one surface through which sperm flows during mating. When retracted into the body at the base of the tail, each half is in a separate "pouch" and is inverted like the pulled out finger of a glove. It is connected to the body by a special muscle that connects at the base and the tip. The presence of the hemipenes in their pouches causes the base of the male's tail to bulge distinctly for several scale rows behind the vent, helping produce the slower taper of the tail compared to a female.

In females there also are pouches just behind the vent, but they are the openings of scent glands that produce chemicals used both for

The rat racer *Spalerosophis diadema* may look like a rat snake at first glance, but look at these eggs! Compare these to the more chicken-egg-shaped eggs of true rat snakes.

R. T. ZAPPALORTI

defense ("musking") and for species identification—snakes are very olfactory animals and many can recognize the sex and species of scent trails long before another snake is seen. The scent gland pouches are shallow compared to hemipenis pouches.

Many advanced keepers use special metal and plastic sticks that taper to narrow points, sex probes, to help determine the sex of small snakes and those that are not obviously of one sex or the other. Probing involves delicately pushing (actually an exaggeration of the force needed) a probe into one of the pouches behind the vent and noting how far in terms of scale rows under the tail that the probe extends before coming to the end of the pouch. Often female scent pouches are only two or three scale rows deep, while male hemipenis pouches may be six or even 12 rows deep. An experienced keeper can evaluate the difference in pouch depth to accurately tell the sex of the snake. This skill is learned by experience, so probing should be learned by watching an experienced keeper do it.

In the wrong hands probes can be

Probing is a delicate procedure that has to be experienced under supervision first. If done incorrectly, you may seriously injure the snake or make it incapable of breeding. Use only probes that are especially manufactured for use with snakes and lizards, never a pencil or a miscellaneous instrument from your old college dissecting kit.

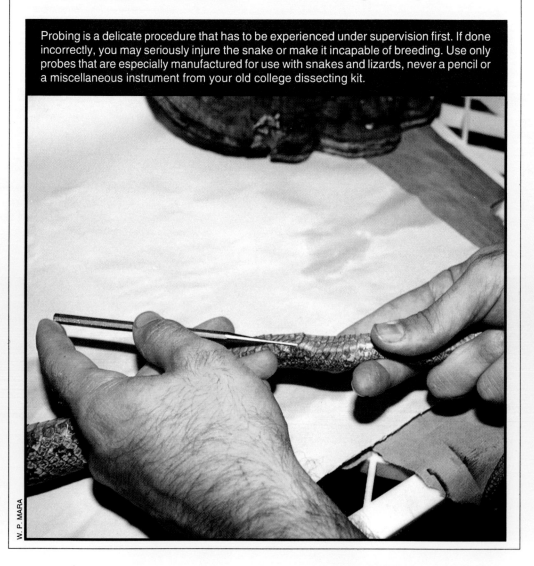

W. P. MARA

R. T. ZAPPALORTI

Notice how the freshly laid eggs of this Corn Snake, *Elaphe guttata guttata*, adhere within minutes of hitting the air. In a natural situation dirt and debris would also adhere to their shells and help camouflage them.

dangerous because they can be pushed in too hard and damage the hemipenis or its muscle. This is a delicate skill, especially when practiced on hatchling or other small snakes.

In rat snakes the longer tail of the male usually means that there are more scale rows under the tail than on the shorter tail of the female. By looking at subcaudal scale counts (as given for most species in Staszko and Walls) for a species, many specimens can be sexed just by counting the pairs of scales under the tail. If the range of counts for the species was expressed as, for instance, 130 to 149, then you could be fairly sure that a specimen with a complete tail and 130 to perhaps 136 scale pairs would be a female, while one with perhaps 143 to 149 would be a male. Specimens with intermediate counts would not be sexable by this method. This is a fast and dirty method that is relatively less stressful to the snake and unlikely to cause damage, and it works well when combined with a visual inspection of tail shape.

CYCLES

For breeding to be successful, almost all rat snakes must be overwintered at a lower than normal

R. D. BARTLETT

A hatchling Tropical Chicken Snake, *Spilotes pullatus*, is a gorgeous animal and very similar to a rat snake at first glance. Though this species can be kept much like a large American Rat Snake (but with a bit warmer and more humid terrarium), it should not be confused with the true rat snakes.

temperature so the sperm of the male, and perhaps the eggs of the female, can mature. There are many physiological processes involved in maturing gonads and sex products, but it seems that in these snakes they all are related to winter hibernation, even in species from the Asian tropics (whose ancestors probably were from cooler climates). Rat snakes are adapted to reduce their activity as the days become shorter and cooler in the fall, become relatively inactive during the about two to five months of winter, and slowly become active as temperatures and daylengths rise during the spring. Tropical rainforest snakes use a different cycle based at least in part on wet and dry seasons, but tropical rat snakes do seem to do well if treated like species from more temperate climates, though further experimentation is in order.

To successfully breed a Corn Snake, American Rat Snake, Four-lined Rat Snake, or most other temperate species, you should begin to reduce the temperature and lighting in perhaps October while slowly reducing feeding as well. Over a period of two or three weeks you should go from the perhaps 80°F

(27°C) and a 12-hour daylength to 50 or 55°F (10 or 13°C) and six hours or less of light per day. Over this same period the snake should be allowed to completely empty the gut. There must always be a water bowl in the cage during the overwintering period, as the snake is not in true hibernation and may continue to drink a bit at intervals. After about three weeks, you can discontinue feeding and turn off the lights, storing the cage in an area that stays at a constant 50°F (10°C) and cannot be invaded by rodents yet stays dark. You are trying to imitate the hibernation den of the rat snake.

Maintain the rat snake in overwintering conditions for at least three weeks, preferably six weeks (and eight won't hurt in most cases). During this time the snake should never become fully active. This means that the temperature in the cage cannot be allowed to rise over 60°F (16°C). Also, you cannot allow the snake to become too cool, so the temperature cannot drop to even 45°F (8°C) during this period. A constant temperature is necessary.

After the six weeks of overwintering, slowly raise the temperature back to normal or a few degrees higher and increase the length of lighting. You'll be going from 50°F (10°C) to about 80 or 85°F (27 or 30°C) and from darkness through six hours of light to about 12 hours over a period of about two weeks. During this time the snake should be allowed to bathe and drink as much as it wants in order to flush waste products from the kidneys. A light meal after the first week should be

Captive-breeding has allowed the commercial production of some truly striking and interesting rat snakes that are seldom or never seen in the wild. This leucistic female Texas Rat Snake, *Elaphe obsoleta lindheimeri*, and her clutch are truly a product of the breeder's art.

J. MERLI

taken, and then the snake should go back to normal.

Only healthy rat snakes can be successfully overwintered. Sick snakes or those that have not been eating will not come out of hibernation. Juveniles can be hibernated (after all, they hibernate in nature) if they have been eating for at least two months before overwintering begins.

MATING

When they come out of overwintering, mature rat snakes (usually three years old, sometimes only two years) should be ready to mate literally on scent. Keep the sexes separate during the two weeks of reconditioning, and then place the male in the female's cage. She will have put her scent over the tank, exciting the male, who will chase her and usually try to grab her behind the head. The pair coil loosely, the female lifts her tail, and the male inserts a hemipenis into the female's vent, where the oviducts accept the sperm. The spines and other projections of the hemipenis allow the male to anchor himself in position during the ten minutes to several hours that are necessary for transfer of sperm. During this time the female may continue to roam about the cage, dragging the male alongside of her. As mating ends she becomes more active, the male disengages, and each snake goes its own way.

Except during breeding, it probably is best to keep rat snake sexes in separate cages if you plan on eventually breeding them. Otherwise males are constantly smelling the tracks left by females and becoming rather confused about which female is ready to mate. Mating usually

One of the more difficult to breed rat snakes is the Trans-Pecos Rat, *Bogertophis subocularis*, but even it has produced unusual varieties, such as this pale or blond phase.

J. MERLI

Hatchlings, like these *Elaphe taeniura ridleyi*, come out of the egg when they are ready. It is not uncommon for a baby to spend the first day of life in the shell after it has been pipped, absorbing energy from the yolk sac and clearing the lung of fluid.

P. FREED

happens at night or in low light. (Use a red or blue light to peek.)

EGGS

About 10 to 12 weeks after mating, the eggs are mature in the female's body and she will lay them in a shallow nest. Many keepers provide a pan of sphagnum moss or potting soil so the female has an appropriate nesting site. If no area of the cage is suitable (proper humidity and temperature, as well as soil texture) for nesting, the female either will hold the eggs inside too long (causing a trip to the veterinarian and possible death of the female) or will lay them at random in the cage (resulting in dead eggs because of rapid drying when exposed to air). The eggs should be removed from the nest, their upper side marked with a soft pencil, and transferred to an incubator. Don't

shake the eggs or rotate them too much, though at this early age the embryo has not yet formed sufficiently to be disturbed if it is rotated in relation to the yolk of the egg.

An incubator can be a complicated commercial model, a plastic shoebox, or just a plastic bowl with a paper towel in the bottom and a tight lid. The object is to keep the eggs at a constant temperature (about 77°F, 25°C) and humidity. The humidity should be just sufficient that water condenses as small droplets on the lid, about 90% or a bit more. A preferred substrate for the incubator is vermiculite, which is clean, holds a great deal of moisture, and cheap. Saturate the vermiculite and then squeeze out the excess water until the vermiculite holds together well yet is not obviously filled with water.

Incubation takes about seven to ten

K. H. SWITAK

Not all eggs in a clutch develop at the same rate, and hatching may occur over a span of several days. Once you have cut open an egg to check it, like these *Elaphe taeniura* eggs, development of the snake inside it probably will stop. If you damage the membranes or the yolk sac, not to mention the embryo itself, you probably will kill the baby. Be patient—you've nothing to lose by waiting a few extra days.

weeks, depending on exact temperature, species, and individual. Most rat snakes have clutches of between 10 and 50 eggs, so be prepared to separate the youngsters as they emerge from the eggs. There is little or no cannibalism in hatchling rat snakes, but if each young is removed to its own small cage it is easier to keep track of proper temperature and humidity and also to see when each young first molts. Between hatching and the first molt, the rat snake baby is surviving on yolk stored in its gut and does not feed (some exceptions). The first meal must be offered as soon as the first molt is over, a crucial period in the young snake's life. Babies from captive-bred strains should feed on

pinkies without any trouble.

OK, that's it. Sex them correctly, overwinter at lower temperatures and short days, be sure the gut is totally empty before overwintering, have water available just in case during overwintering, keep the sexes separate until mating, allow the female to find a good place to put her eggs, incubate properly, and *voi la*, babies. Corn Snakes perhaps are the best species to start with for breeding experience, but Yellow Rat Snakes and other species with long histories in captivity also are good for the beginner. If in doubt, check with an experienced local breeder (usually someone at the pet shop will know such as person) or vet who specializes in snakes. Have fun!

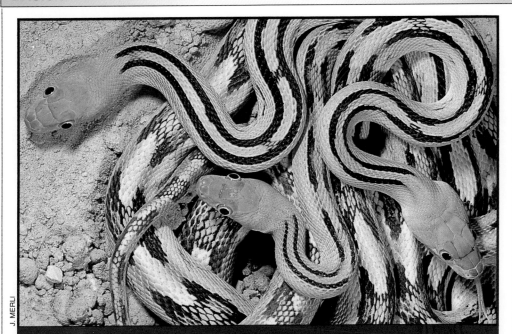

J. MERLI

Above: Captive breeding of unusual and rare rat snakes may make them available to the average hobbyist. Few Trans-Pecos Rat Snakes, *Bogertophis subocularis,* would be available today if we had to depend on wild-caught specimens. **Below:** These *Elaphe schrencki* are hatching from really filthy eggs. Remember that in nature the dirt and debris adhering to the shells help camouflage them and may actually improve their ability to retain the correct moisture. Even chicken eggs often are filthy when laid, but that does not stop them from hatching. Nature is a wonderful biologist who knows just when a little dirt is good for her children.

S. KOCHETOV

R. T. ZAPPALORTI

If you look very closely you can just make out the egg tooth of this hatching Black Rat Snake, *Elaphe obsoleta obsoleta*, under the rostral scale. The tooth is a transient structure fixed loosely to the upper jaw and will be shed within hours of hatching. Even some livebearing snakes still produce young with egg teeth.

AMERICAN RATS AND CORNS

Five species of typical rat snakes, genus *Elaphe*, are found in the United States and northern Mexico. The one every snake keeper knows is, of course, the Corn Snake, *Elaphe guttata*, a very popular species bred in many different colors and patterns. The American Rat Snake, *Elaphe obsoleta*, occurs as four fairly distinct subspecies, all bred for the hobby, and some more doubtful entities, while the other two species found mostly in the United States, the Fox Snake (*Elaphe vulpina*) and Baird's Rat Snake (*Elaphe bairdi*), are not especially popular in the pet shops. The fifth species, the unusual Nightsnake or Mexican Rat Snake, *Elaphe flavirufa*, is virtually unknown to hobbyists. These species are all covered in detail in *Rat Snakes* by Staszko and Walls, and I won't even

Staszko and Walls. *Rat Snakes.* T.F.H. TS-144. Available at your local pet shop.

Not a striking beauty, Baird's Rat Snake, *Elaphe bairdi*, has only a limited following in the hobby.

W. P. MARA

W. P. MARA

Even a relatively plain rat snake can have touches of beauty. In Baird's Rat Snake, *Elaphe bairdi*, there usually is at least a trace of orangish buff color on the belly. Under the supervision of captive breeders, it has been possible to exaggerate the orange of some breeding lines until it creeps up the sides of the snake and even begins to show in the back pattern. This particular specimen is of a rather poorly colored lineage in which the usual brown stripes of the back have almost disappeared but the orange of the belly is not very obvious on the sides or back.

W. P. MARA

P. H. BRIGGS, COURTESY L. LEMKE

The Nightsnake, *Elaphe flavirufa*, is a poorly understood Mexican rat snake that seldom is kept in captivity. Notice the way the dorsal saddles tend to fuse to produce a pattern of broken zig-zags over part of the back. It seems that with careful breeding such a character possibly could be exaggerated to produce a very attractive snake, but so far few keepers have had much success breeding the Nightsnake.

attempt to cover the details of identification and natural history here. Instead, we'll look mostly at the American Rat Snake and the Fox Snake and just touch on the Corn Snake.

CORN SNAKES

An entire book could be written on this species—and in fact several have—but I'll only give it a few paragraphs because the species is covered in more detail in a separate title of this series. Suffice it to say that the Corn Snake, *Elaphe guttata*, is a medium-sized, rather slender snake that averages about 3 feet in length but reaches over 4 feet on occasion. It is some shade of tan to creamy tan or reddish tan above, with squarish saddles of bright reddish brown to red over the back and a distinct spearpoint on the head ending between the eyes. The broad stripe running from the eye to the corner of the mouth is reddish and has black borders. The Corn Snake occurs over all the southeastern United States, ranging from New Jersey to the tip of Florida and

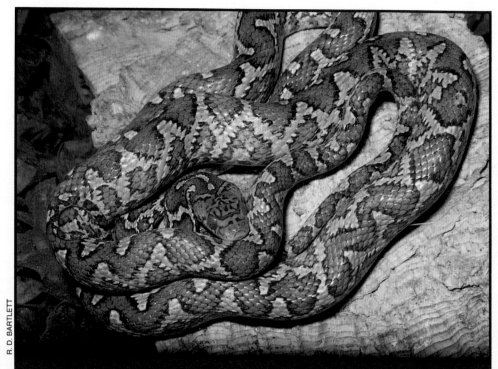

R. D. BARTLETT

Two American rat snakes of rather limited hobby interest are the Nightsnake, *Elaphe flavirufa*, of Mexico and points south (top) and the Great Plains Rat Snake, *Elaphe guttata emoryi*, of the drier central prairie of the United States.

W. P. MARA

westward to Louisiana and Illinois. In southern Florida it often develops unusual patterns and has been given different names not recognized by most herpetologists today, while west of the Mississippi River it is replaced by a very similar snake, the Great Plains Rat Snake, that traditionally has been treated as a subspecies, *E. guttata emoryi.* Today several 81°F (27°C) or so, at least ten hours of light per day, a warm basking area, and a water bowl. They don't especially enjoy climbing, so branches are unnecessary, as are plants. Captive-bred specimens, the only type worth buying, are cheap even as albinos and other color varieties, and feed readily on pinkie and fuzzy mice, sometimes even

W. P. MARA

Albino Corn Snakes, *Elaphe guttata guttata*, come in several minor varieties, some more attractive than others. This "Creamsicle" Corn is one of the most brilliant of the albinos.

scientists feel that this form should instead be treated as a full species because there are very few areas where intermediates are found. The Great Plains Rat Snake is much like a brownish Corn Snake but otherwise is like the Corn in keepability, though it tolerates drier conditions and warmer temperatures. Few hobbyists keep *E. g. emoryi* because of its rather dull coloration, but it does make an excellent pet.

Corn Snakes thrive in captivity if given a fairly dry terrarium kept at adult mice. This is one of the easiest snakes to maintain in captivity, and commercial breeders produce literally thousands each year. *There is no reason for the beginner to ever buy or collect a wild Corn Snake.*

Breeding Corn Snakes is easy, as you would expect. Overwinter your adults at 50 to 60°F (10 to 16°C) for at least one month as explained earlier and then place them together to breed in the spring. Some 10 to 15 (often more) eggs are laid in a clutch and hatch in two to three months. The young usually will take pinkie

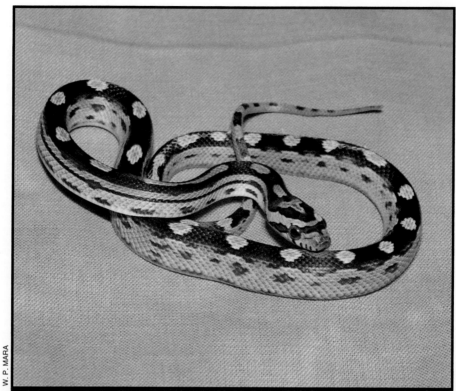

W. P. MARA

Breeders produce more Corn Snakes, *Elaphe guttata guttata*, than any other single species of snake, and they produce them in many major and minor color varieties. The oddly patterned Corn above is dubbed the Hurricane Corn Snake, while the interesting albino below is a Candy Cane variety.

W. P. MARA

mice as soon as they complete their first molt. You can't go wrong with a Corn Snake!

THE AMERICAN RAT SNAKE

For a century American herpetologists have been in love with the subspecies concept, the idea that when a distinctive color pattern or

ones plus a half-dozen less distinct forms that most scientists no longer recognize as valid but hobbyists still keep and like to name.

The American Rat Snake, *Elaphe obsoleta*, ranges over the entire eastern half of the United States east of the Great Plains and even enters Canada (and just a little bit of

W. P. MARA

In this strain or lineage of Corn Snake the red and yellow coloration has been lost, producing basically a two-toned snake. Such specimens are often called melanistic (though this is technically incorrect) or black albinos.

scale count occurs in a restricted part of the range of a species, that segment of the species should get its own name as a subspecies. Often subspecies have led to gigantic misunderstandings of species as living animals, and seldom have they helped solve any biological problems. Today the pendulum has swung away from subspecies, but American hobbyists still insist on using subspecies names for the animals they keep. In the American Rat Snake, *Elaphe obsoleta*, there are subspecies to spare, four distinct

northeastern Mexico), so obviously it is an adaptable species. This works to its advantage in the terrarium, as it tolerates a broad array of keeping conditions as long as the terrarium is not too wet or dry and not excessively warm or cold. In other words, it keeps well at normal room temperatures and humidities almost anywhere. Provide it with a basking rock and at least eight hours of light per day and it will do fine. In captivity it feeds well on mice and chicks and even will take eggs (another common name for this species is Chicken Snake in much of the southern U.S.). Like most rat snakes, specimens often reach ten years in captivity and may exceed 20 on occasion.

In nature, American Rat Snakes, especially the northeastern subspecies *Elaphe obsoleta obsoleta,*

snakes have male combat rituals as well, including some of the *Pituophis* species and the kingsnakes.

Mating occurs in the spring after hibernation, and eggs are laid about six weeks later. Clutches may be quite large, three or four dozen eggs,

R. D. BARTLETT

Perhaps the meanest American Rat Snake, the Texas Rat, *Elaphe obsoleta lindheimeri,* of western Louisiana and eastern Texas has an undistinguished and usually rather dull pattern. In the right hands, however, it has produce some truly excellent color varieties that are very popular. The varieties, incidentally, tend to be as mean as the normal form.

commonly called the Black Rat Snake because adults are mostly deep brown to almost black, hiding the saddles of the juvenile, are noted for male combat rituals, where two males fight by coiling about each other for sometimes several hours, trying to pin each other to the ground. Such fighting has been assumed to be territorial fights or fights over mating rights, but there is little real evidence to support either possibility. Other

the young emerging about three months (as little as 50 days, as much as 110) later. Captive-bred strains usually feed as soon as they finish their first molt and will take the usual pinkies as well as small eggs and even fish.

If you don't mind a large (commonly 5 feet long and may reach over 8 feet) and fairly aggressive snake, the American Rat Snake makes a fine pet. The southeastern subspecies, which are tan to yellowish or even bright orange with narrow brown stripes (*E. obsoleta quadrivittata*, the Yellow Rat Snake, as well as the doubtful orange *E. o. rossalleni*), are captive-bred in large numbers and are readily available. As in the young of all American Rat Snakes, for the first year or so of life the snakes have brown saddles on a paler background, but in the Yellow Rat Snake the saddles soon begin to connect at the corners to produce stripes, while the saddles themselves fade and eventually disappear, leaving just the stripes. Yellow Rat Snakes are relatively tame snakes, sometimes very colorful, and do extremely well in captivity, making them prime rat snakes for the beginner.

The other subspecies, including the brown northeastern *E. o. obsoleta* as well as the two southern subspecies (*E. o. spiloides* and *E. o. lindheimeri*) that retain the juvenile saddles throughout life, are not as popular because of more subdued coloration and often more aggressive temperament. In fact, the Texas Rat Snake, *E. o. lindheimeri*, is considered by many collectors to be one of the most aggressive North American snakes, and it often does not calm down in captivity.

Next to the Corn Snake, the Yellow Rat Snake is the most often-sold rat snake and the most commonly bred.

An albino (note the red eye) Black Rat Snake, *Elaphe obsoleta obsoleta*. Few keepers like the dull brown to bright black normal form of this subspecies, but the various albinistic varieties have developed quite a following.

W. P. MARA

W. P. MARA

The Yellow Rat Snake, *Elaphe obsoleta quadrivittata*, probably is the most popular subspecies of the American Rat Snake. Many specimens are very attractive shades of yellow or at least bright tan, but some (such as the one below) tend more toward an unattractive olive green.

R. D. BARTLETT

It is available at most pet shops that handle snakes and is easy to get through dealer lists. Recently, however, several new strains of the Black Rat Snake have been developed, including a truly beautiful alabaster albino form, and it has become more available. The southern subspecies *E. o. lindheimeri*, the Texas Rat Snake, though not attractive and certainly mean in the natural form, has produced two striking white strains that are becoming quite available at moderate prices. One is a fairly typical albino or near-albino, technically amelanistic, with reddish eyes and sometimes faint traces of pattern, but the other is an alabaster, opaque white leucistic form with blue eyes. Any of these captive-bred strains, if priced right, should make good pets.

FOX SNAKES

Though it is not commonly available, at least not as captive-bred specimens, the elegant Fox Snake, *Elaphe vulpina*, of the Great Lakes and upper Midwest area has excellent potential as a gentle, hardy pet

M. SMITH

The young of all subspecies of American Rat Snake, *Elaphe obsoleta*, have a similar pattern of dark saddles on a grayish or tan background and an incomplete head pattern as compared to a Corn Snake.

R. D. BARTLETT

An attractive color variety of *Elaphe obsoleta quadrivittata* from Florida. Notice the similarity to the *Elaphe obsoleta rossalleni* shown on the facing page.

snake. Usually 3 feet long as an adult, it has the typical Corn Snake-like pattern of brownish dorsal saddles, but the head is often a bright reddish brown above while the throat and neck may be bright yellow. Though it can be kept like the Corn Snake or American Rat Snake, breeding is more difficult because this species needs a long hibernation of at least two months to mature the sperm. Also, the species is under a great deal of pressure from habitat destruction over much of its range, and in some areas where once abundant it now is uncommon or rare.

This species has gained a reputation as a very gentle species that virtually never bites once it adjusts to captivity. Additionally, a legend has developed that it is fast to release its scent glands, but this is refuted by many keepers. The common name has been stated to be based on the fox-red color of the head or the supposedly fox-like scent of the scent glands (also refuted by many keepers), but it also has been suggested that the scientific name

A beautiful orange specimen of the Everglades Rat Snake, *Elaphe obsoleta rossalleni*. This subspecies is at best weakly distinguished from the Yellow Rat Snake, whose range surrounds it.

P. H. BRIGGS, COURTESY L. LEMKE

Above: This oddly patterned juvenile belongs to the Florida variety of *Elaphe obsoleta* sometimes called *williamsi*. **Below:** Fox Snakes, *Elaphe vulpina*, are sometimes very attractive snakes with all the brilliance of a Corn Snake. Notice the virtual absence of a head pattern in this specimen, typical of the species.

vulpina, which means "fox," is actually based on the name of the collector of one of the type specimens, Reverend Charles Fox. With luck, captive-bred strains of Reverend Fox's snake will survive into the next century even if the species should disappear from the wild.

pattern. Most specimens are rather plain brown with brown stripes, but one strain has a bright orange belly and lower sides, sometimes with the orange extending onto the head and even brightening-up the stripes of the back as well. If you want to try a specimen or two, they can be kept

W. P. MARA

Many Fox Snakes have bright red or orange heads and bright yellow on the throat and lower sides just behind the head. One of the more interesting species of neglected rat snakes, the Fox is not always easy to care for.

THE OTHERS

Recently Baird's Rat Snake, *Elaphe bairdi*, a species of dry canyons, prairies, and oak knolls of southern Texas and adjacent Mexico, has entered the hobby in small numbers. This striped species looks much like a Yellow Rat Snake of the brownish variety from the Carolinas, but differs from *Elaphe obsoleta* in several rather variable characters of scalation and

much like Corn Snakes.

The Nightsnake or Mexican Rat Snake, *Elaphe flavirufa*, at first glance looks like a Corn Snake both in color and pattern, but the saddles on the back often fuse into broad, broken zig-zags. There is no spearpoint on the top of the head, which should prevent confusion with any Corn Snake variant. This is a mostly nocturnal rat snake that reaches over 5 feet in length and can be kept much like a Corn Snake, tolerating higher temperatures. The pattern is quite variable, and five subspecies have been described, one of which (*E. f. phaescens* of the Yucatan) often is considered to be a full species. Though the Nightsnake has been kept in captivity on occasion, it is a rare and poorly known species that is almost unavailable to the average hobbyist. There have been suggestions that, though it superficially resembles the Corn Snake, the Nightsnake should form its own genus, for which the name *Pseudoelaphe* is available. However, it would take a lot of detailed work to show that such a genus was truly distinct and worth recognizing as different from *Elaphe*.

Three other rat snakes are found in North America, but they are no longer in the genus *Elaphe* and will be treated in later chapters as "brownies" and "greenies" for the genera *Bogertophis* and *Senticolis*.

American rat snakes are just varied enough to be interesting, and they become even more interesting as captive-bred variants of the Corn Snake and recently the American Rat Snake have entered the market at reasonable prices. However, they are not nearly as diverse as the 30 species of rat snakes from Europe and Asia, some of which we'll briefly cover in the next chapter.

The head pattern of *Elaphe bimaculata* of Asia is at first glance similar to that of the American Corn Snake, but probably this spearhead pattern is a primitive character of rat snakes retained from an ancestor.

W. P. MARA

EURASIAN RATS

Asia, especially the mountainous regions of southern China and northern Southeast Asia to India, is where rat snakes really come into their own. Because of the politics of this area and the often difficult terrain, this has meant that many species restricted to this "rat snake homeland" have not entered the hobby and are virtually unknown in the terrarium. In many cases these species also are almost unknown as to their natural history, with only a few lines being published or, in several cases, nothing having reached the literature.

Thirty species of *Elaphe* are found in Europe and Asia. Two bright green species are treated in the chapter on "greenies," *E. frenata* and *E. prasina*. The following species are unknown or very rare in the hobby at present and will not be treated further:

Elaphe cantoris, Eastern Trinket Snake: Sikkim to Burma.

Elaphe conspicillata, Red Japanese Rat Snake: Southern Japan.

Elaphe davidi, Pere David's Rat Snake: Northeastern China.

Elaphe dione, Steppes Rat Snake: Caspian Sea to Korea.

Elaphe hodgsoni, Himalayan Rat Snake: Kasmir, Nepal, Sikkim, Assam.

Elaphe hohenackeri, Transcaucasian Rat Snake: Turkey and vicinity.

Elaphe japonica, Northern Japanese Rat Snake: Northern Japan.

Elaphe leonardi, Burmese Rat Snake: Northern Burma to Vietnam and adjacent China.

Elaphe perlacea, Szechwan Rat

Recently a few captive-bred specimens of the Twin-spotted Rat Snake, *Elaphe bimaculata*, have appeared on the market. This attractive, small, easy to keep rat snake could eventually prove to be a staple of the hobby if enough people begin to breed it.

W. P. MARA

Snake: Southeastern China.

Elaphe quadrivirgata, Japanese Four-lined Rat Snake: Japan.

Elaphe subradiata, Sunda Rat Snake: Eastern Indonesia.

This still leaves a lot of species to cover in just a few pages, so if you want more detailed information you will have to refer to Staszko and Walls, *Rat Snakes*, for longer discussions. Here we'll just skim the surface of the ten or so species actually now in the hobby and several similar species.

EUROPEAN RAT SNAKES

Four rat snakes are found in Europe, but only one (*E. scalaris*, Ladder Rat Snake) is restricted to Europe, where it is found over much of the Iberian Peninsula (i.e., Spain and Portugal) and southern France. Adults have two very closely placed brown stripes on the back and a strong stripe back from the eye, while juveniles have short, narrow blotches connecting the stripes and vaguely resembling a ladder. The long rostral scale projects back to partially divide

Only the specialist breeder is likely to try to keep the Stinking Goddess. Though an attractive species, it has many disadvantages of both behavior and natural history that probably will keep it from ever becoming popular.

R. D. BARTLETT

P. H. BRIGGS, COURTESY L. LEMKE

Kunisir Island Rats, more properly the Japanese Rat Snake, *Elaphe climacophora*, are bred in captivity but are not especially distinctive or attractive. Certainly they never will replace the Corn Snake as a major hobby rat snake interest, but they may prove to be very adaptable snakes that could throw interesting color varieties.

the internasal scales on top of the snout, a very unusual character in rat snakes.

The Aesculapian Rat Snake, *Elaphe longissima*, is found over much of temperate Europe and even has colonies in Germany and other more northern areas, where it may have been introduced by the Roman legions during their movements over 20 centuries ago. This species always has been associated with man, and it is the species that appears on the medical staff emblem. Though it likes warm, dry, Mediterranean climates, it obviously is quite adaptable. Its juvenile has two bright yellowish creamy spots behind the head that persist after the blotched body pattern is replaced by the stripes of the adult. These pale nape blotches are thought to be involved in some type of mimicry with the Grass Snake, *Natrix natrix*, but I've seen no detailed discussion of this and don't know which is supposed to be the model and which the mimic.

Only the Four-lined Rat Snake, *Elaphe quatuorlineata*, is present in any numbers in the terrarium hobby. This is a widely distributed species typical of dry regions around the

Two rat snakes not common in the hobby are the Steppes Rat Snake, *Elaphe dione* (top), and the Four-lined Rat Snake, *Elaphe quatuorlineata*. These Asian and Eurasian species are more likely to be seen on the European market than in America, but neither is commonly bred in captivity. If you look hard enough you might find a Four-lined, however.

W. P. MARA

A juvenile *Elaphe quatuorlineata muenteri*, one of the Mediterranean island subspecies of the Four-lined Rat Snake.

Caspian Sea in western Asia, the species extending westward over the Mediterranean region and the Balkans as far west as Italy. In most of its European range it looks much like a brown Yellow Rat Snake (*Elaphe obsoleta quadrivittata*), having four dark brown stripes, but there also is a broad dark brown stripe from the eye to the angle of the jaw that usually is absent in the Yellow Rat Snake. In the eastern part of its range it tends to retain the juvenile blotched pattern into the adults, as represented by the subspecies *E. q. sauromates*, which sometimes is available. Don't worry too much about subspecies in this species as the several described forms from Mediterranean islands are unrecognizable by hobbyists—and probably by expert herpetologists as well.

All three of these typical European rat snakes are fairly large, heavy-bodied snakes that often reach 3 to 4 feet in length and in general appearance and ecology seem to be very similar to the American Rat Snake, *Elaphe obsoleta*. They can be kept much like that species and reproduce similarly in captivity, though the incubation period of the warm-adapted Ladder and Four-lined Rat Snakes may be as little as four or five weeks in some cases. All like to bask and must be overwintered for consistently successful breeding.

LEOPARDS AND ALLIES

A group of about a half dozen rather small (often under 3 feet), slender, spotted rat snakes is centered about the Caspian Sea and the high plateaus of western Asia, with some species being found east into eastern-most China and even Siberia. This group of similarly patterned species (though not necessarily biologically related) includes such uncommon species as *Elaphe hohenackeri* and *E. dione*, as well as the more familiar *E. situla* (Leopard Rat Snake) and *E.*

The Leopard Rat Snake, *Elaphe situla*, is one of the most attractive small Eurasian rats and one of the most desirable. It it difficult to keep for long in captivity, however, and seldom is bred.

bimaculata (Twin-spotted Rat Snake). Also similar is the nearly aquatic, live-bearing, cold-adapted Chinese Gartersnake, *Elaphe rufodorsata*, a fish- and frog-eating species from Korea and adjacent areas. These are among the most beautiful rat snakes, in many ways resembling the Corn Snake in general appearance, though usually the dorsal saddles in these species are actually pairs of spots that tend to fuse across the middle of the back. Often the background is bright yellow, the spots reddish brown and in high contrast. There commonly is a spearpoint on top of the head and broad black-edged bands on the side of the head.

All require a rather long overwintering to successfully reproduce, and in some cases the incubation period is very short, not uncommonly less than a month, a response to harsh climates. They like to bask and can be kept much like Corn Snakes, though they will tolerate much cooler temperatures, often as low as 68°F (20°C) for the Twin-spotted Rat and Chinese Gartersnake. The Leopard Rat Snake is considered by European hobbyists among the most desirable of the rats because it is found in western Europe, is rare or uncommon, and has been greatly reduced in numbers by loss of habitat. It is not an easy species to keep or breed, however, and the beginning hobbyist with a touch for unusual and beautiful rat snakes would be well advised to look for a Twin-spotted Rat Snake instead, a species often now seen as captive-bred specimens.

STRIPE-TAILED RAT SNAKES

Elaphe taeniura, often called the Taiwan Beauty Snake as well as the Stripe-tailed Rat Snake, is one of the trinket snakes, rat snakes with very simple head patterns and usually stripes on the body. It is one of the most simply marked species of the group, with the head and neck virtually unpatterned except for a broad dark stripe from the eye to the back of the head along the upper edges of the lip scales (not angling down to the corner of the mouth). Though the center of the back is sometimes unmarked or has a broad yellowish or clay-colored stripe, on the front part of the body the pairs of small dark blotches on each side of the back sometimes fuse to produce "butterfly" spots on the neck. The pattern is exceeding variable, leading to the recognition of many poorly described subspecies, but in all the subspecies and variants the tail is strongly striped with dark brown and yellowish, a feature that when combined with the head pattern is distinctive.

This is a big (often 6 feet long) snake with a mean temper, factors that have not aided its popularity. However, it is very adaptable, occurring in varied habitats over much of eastern and southeastern Asia. Very pale specimens with pearly

Stripe-tailed Rat Snakes, *Elaphe taeniura*, have recently been imported in some numbers. These attractive but large and often mean rat snakes now are being bred in small numbers but still are not easy to obtain.

J. MERLI

white stripes are found in caves in southern Asia, one of the stranger adaptations of the rat snakes. It feeds on a broad variety of mammals and birds and also is fed upon by man. This is the most commonly eaten snake in southern Asia, where thousands appear in the markets for food, medicine (especially the gall bladder), and leather.

As a pet the Stripe-tail makes a hardy specimen for the large terrarium and can be kept much like the American Rat Snake, liking a temperature around 84°F (29°C), half-day lighting, and a nice warm basking rock. It climbs well and enjoys sturdy climbing branches. Recently it has been bred in small numbers and has become more available on the market, though it still is far from common. If you can get a captive-bred young specimen that takes frozen and thawed mice, you should have an excellent and beautiful snake. If you try to breed this species, ignore the subspecific names you see on the lists and try to breed only pairs with virtually identical patterns or from the same known locality in order to keep pure lineages.

TRINKETS

The group of species clustered around the Indian *Elaphe helena*, the Common Trinket Snake, for some reason is poorly represented in the terrarium hobby. These are beautiful though simply patterned snakes, usually some 3 feet long, with narrow heads and usually strong dark lines down and back from the eye and, typically, paired stripes on the nape

A gorgeous yellow hatchling of the Common Trinket Snake, *Elaphe helena*, shows what a hobbyist who sticks to just the most common species might be missing. However, beginners should hone their skills on the more common species first before trying the odder ones.

R. D. BARTLETT

Though plain in coloration, the Reddish Rat Snake, *Elaphe erythrura*, is imported from the Philippines on occasion. Certainly the color is unique in the true rat snakes.

R. D. BARTLETT

of the neck. Most species have reddish heads, resulting in many local common names involving the term "copperhead." Included here, among others, are the Reddish Rat Snake, *E. erythrura*, of the Philippines and Celebes, often just a plain bright reddish brown overall with only traces of head pattern; the Black Copper Rat Snake, *E. flavolineata*, of southeastern Asia and Indonesia, with a bright yellow midback stripe and a head pattern of two dark lines from the eye and a heavy line on the lower nape; and the gorgeous Black-banded Trinket Snake, *E. porphyracea*, from much of southeastern Asia, which has narrow black rings over the back and three narrow black stripes on top of the head. The Common Trinket Snake, *E. helena*, has pairs of small white-centered blotches along the back and a pair of broad dark stripes on the nape, with an obvious second pair of dark stripes on the side of the neck. In almost all the species of trinket snakes the tail has dark brown stripes along the sides and is bright brown to yellowish above.

Trinket snakes in general are gentle species that feed well on small mammals and birds, like the light and basking, and may not need an overwintering period to reproduce in captivity. Unfortunately they seldom are bred in captivity and are not imported on a regular basis either, though they may be very common in nature and are eaten by local residents. Many species come from mountainous regions so are hard to collect for the hobby. This also means that they can tolerate fairly low temperatures in the terrarium. If you see any trinket snake that is in good condition (preferably captive-bred) and reasonably priced you might want to give it a try, but first have your veterinarian look it over and treat it for the various internal parasites it is sure to have. Trinket snakes have a lot of potential for the hobby, and it is only a matter of time until one or more species become popular.

RADIATED RAT SNAKES

The rather odd trinket snake *Elaphe radiata*, the Radiated Rat Snake, is in general appearance much like a Stripe-tailed Rat Snake

P. H. BRIGGS, COURTESY L. LEMKE

The Black Copper Rat Snake, *Elaphe flavolineata*, is an interesting Southeast Asian species that for some reason seldom is imported. Perhaps there is a stronger market for its skin and flesh than for living specimens.

but with a more complicated head pattern including a narrow band over the nape connecting two narrow black lines from the eyes over the back of the head, as well as two lines down and back from each eye. In most respects of captivity it is much like *E. taeniura*, a large species (5 feet and more) that likes the light and feeds on small mammals and birds. However, its hemipenes are very unusual for a rat snake and it has been suggested that it (and perhaps some of the other trinket snakes) should be placed in a distinct genus, for which the name *Coelognathus* is available; in fact, recently a few authors have used this generic name for the Radiated Rat, even though full details for the separation of the genus have not been published. This is a good though aggressive species in the terrarium and deserves more attention from hobbyists as it appears on the market with some regularity, always wild-caught.

SOME ODDBALLS

I'm running out of room but have to find a place for a few lines on five species that are seen on the market with some regularity and are distinctive though somewhat difficult terrarium species. The Stinking Goddess, *Elaphe carinata*, of eastern China has strongly keeled scales, a slightly vertical pupil of the eye, and a bright yellow and black pattern especially conspicuous on the head, where each scale is outlined in black. A small scale is lodged between the eye and the upper lip scales, an uncommon feature in the rat snakes. The scent glands are extremely potent in this odd species. At 5 feet in length, it is a large, aggressive (very mean actually) species that prefers to feed on snakes and lizards, taking mammals and birds only when forced. It differs in so many features from typical rat snakes that it has been suggested it be placed in its own genus, for which the old name *Phyllophis* seems to be available. A few wild-caught specimens are around in the hobby, but it is a difficult species that has proved very hard to breed.

The Red-headed Rat Snake, *Elaphe moellendorffi*, is a beautiful snake that appears occasionally in the hobby but is almost never bred. It is large (usually 5 or 6 feet long) but rather gentle and likes cool temperatures seldom exceeding 70°F (21°C). In good specimens the head is bright red on top, the back is gray with reddish brown blotches, and the tail is bright red. It has an elongated head with a long snout that gives it a very distinctive aspect. A native of eastern China, this was a very rare snake until the 1960's, and even today it still is not well-known. Eggs have hatched in about nine weeks at 81°F (27°C), but the species seldom survives well in captivity, so far.

Three far-northern rat snakes currently are fairly available in the hobby and have their fans. One, the Mandarin Rat Snake, *Elaphe mandarina*, is a spectacular yellow, black, and brown species with a brightly striped head and red stripes on the scales. An eastern Chinese species, it is small (usually under 3 feet) and nocturnal, liking a cool (75°F, 24°C), dark, quiet cage with few disturbances. The Japanese Rat Snake, *Elaphe climacophora*, is a rather blandly patterned snake from Japan that recently has been bred in small numbers from a population coming from Kunisir Island in the Russian Arctic. It needs a long overwintering period and is slow to become sexually mature (four years). An interesting species, but one that

Red-headed Rat Snakes, *Elaphe moellendorffi*, is one of the most beautiful rat snakes. Virtually unknown just 25 years ago, today it often appears on the pet market.

R. D. BARTLETT

R. D. BARTLETT

Recently Mandarin Rat Snakes, *Elaphe mandarina*, have been bred in small numbers. One of the most unusually colored rat snakes, these animals like it cool.

probably is not fated to take the hobby by storm. In a similar position is the Amur Rat Snake, *Elaphe schrencki*, of northeastern Russia and adjacent China. This is a big (5 feet and more), heavy-bodied snake that comes in two subspecies, both available on the market as captive-bred specimens, though far from common. It likes to climb, likes a cool cage (not much over 75°F, 24°C), and needs a very long overwintering period of as much as five months to produce viable egg clutches. This can be a difficult species to keep, probably because it is kept too warm, but several hobbyists have had good luck with it. Though not brightly colored, the Amur Rat Snake is interesting in its own way and worth getting if you can find a captive-bred specimen at a reasonable price.

These few pages obviously cannot start to do justice to the Asian rat snakes, but I hope they will give you at least an idea of the variety and beauty of the obscure species that occasionally reach us from the jungles and mountains of a poorly understood region. Perhaps some day one or more of these species will become hobby standards, which can only serve to increase interest in the hobby.

THE GREENIES

There are many green snakes found in the different faunas of the world, and they are placed in many different genera and even families. The four snakes we are concerned with in this chapter belong to three different genera, and only one of the species is at all common in the hobby. In other words, this is a real jumble of a chapter heading and I did it just to get some of the species out of the previous chapters, which were running too long. Ah, the tribulations of the poor author!

ASIAN GREENS

OK, serious now. Two species of bright green *Elaphe* occur in the cool mountains of southern Asia. *Elaphe frenata*, the Assam Green Trinket Snake, often is over 4 feet long, bright green above and pale green below, with a dark line through the eye and the back of the head. The snout is rather long, and often the rostral scale is a bit produced and the internasal scales may be fused, while the loreal scale before the eye is fused with the prefrontal, all rather unusual characters in the genus. It ranges in a band from Assam through southern China and is very poorly known, with few observations on its natural history. The other green rat snake, *Elaphe prasina*, the Green Trinket Snake, is a bit smaller (to about 4 feet maximum) and has an unmarked head with the normal snout and head scales for the group. It also is bright green above and paler green below. A bit more tropical than its Assam cousin, it ranges from Assam southeast through parts of Burma and southern China into the higher elevations of Thailand, Cambodia, Laos, and Vietnam. Neither of these species is currently available on the market as far as I can tell, and even the European literature has almost no data on keeping them alive in captivity. They have always been considered rare species, very hard to see in their natural habitat, and political conditions in their home areas have been unstable for over a century. Assumedly they could be kept in a tall, rather cool and humid terrarium with many climbing branches and subdued light. They should take mice, though lizards might be expected to be part of the diet of *E. frenata* because of the snout modifications. I guess they are egg-layers (actually, I've seen no confirmation of this), and they probably have short incubation periods because of the harsh climatic conditions.

Recently these two species have been referred to the genus *Gonyosoma* by Dr. H. Dowling in a checklist of Burmese snakes, a relationship once suggested because of the similar color patterns of the two species and the Red-tailed Rat Snake, the type species of *Gonyosoma*. However, over 35 years ago Dr. Dowling addressed the relationships of these same three species and came to the conclusion that they shared only a green color pattern and differed in many structural characters, so he firmly put *frenata* and *prasina* back into *Elaphe*. Because I've seen no detailed reasons published for a change, I'm leaving these three species where Dr. Dowling placed them back in 1958.

MANGROVE MEANY

The Red-tailed Rat Snake, *Gonyosoma oxycephalum*, is found on the market on occasion, but it has a

R. D. BARTLETT

Beautiful but mean, most beginners would be best not trying a Red-tailed Rat Snake, *Gonyosoma oxycephalum*, until they had more experience for far tamer species.

poor reputation. Often called the Red-tailed Green Rat Snake or the Mangrove Rat Snake, it might just as well be called the Super Mean Rat Snake. The head is elongated, the eyes are protuberant, and the tail is very long, all adaptations to a tree-climbing lifestyle and a propensity for plucking birds out of the air if they come too close, much like an Emerald Tree Boa (also, curiously, a green snake noted for its mean temper). The snake undoubtedly is a beautiful species, bright green to yellow green above, bright yellow below, with the top of the head mahogany brown and the tail bright red, often with a narrow yellow line separating the tail color from the body color. The broad black line through the eye and the back of the head separates the brown top of the head from bright yellow-green lip scales. Recently some very unusually patterned specimens have been imported from Indonesia, these often brightly blotched with yellow on a gray or brown background color, sometimes with the entire head bright yellow. Although the name *janseni* has been applied by hobbyists to these snakes, it is best for the moment to just consider them odd *G. oxycephalum*. The Red-tail is an abundant species in the humid lowlands of all of Southeast Asia, including Indonesia and the Celebes.

Hobbyists seldom have had good luck with this beautiful snake, perhaps because wild-caught specimens (the only ones currently available) have been mishandled, are very stressed, and probably have a tremendous number of intestinal worms and other parasites. First, take your specimen to a vet and have it put though a course of worming. Second, pay your vet extra for the wounds inflicted during worming. Third, buy plenty of iodine and adhesive bandages. Fourth, maybe you'd be better off with a Corn Snake.

Anyway, the Red-tail needs a tall, heavily planted (plastic plants and firmly anchored branches will do) terrarium that can be kept at about 90°F (32°C) and nearly 100% humidity, the temperature not dropping below 75°F (24°C) even at night. The snake will spend all its time curled on the branches and seldom will come to the ground. Mist the cage and the snake daily to help maintain the humidity. Beware of possible fungal and bacterial growth on the tank and the substrate. The Red-tail may reach 7.5 feet in length and commonly is over 5 feet, so you need a large terrarium for this species. Feed chicks and mice, but be prepared for poor feeders. Supposedly this species takes bird eggs, like the American Rat Snake. This is not an easy snake to maintain, and when combined with its evil temper only the dedicated hobbyist is likely to put up with it.

Although seldom bred in captivity, a few captive-bred or at least captive-hatched specimens show up occasionally, mostly the offspring of gravid females laying in captivity. Six to eight eggs are laid in a clutch and they hatch in about three to four months if kept at 82°F (28°C). The young are 18 inches or so in length and have been seen to eat frogs and lizards in nature. Sexual maturity may take four years, so it can be expected that healthy adults live long lives in nature, even though short-lived in captivity.

The exact relationships of the Red-tailed Rat Snake to the other rat snakes is uncertain. Many features of its skeleton would seem to indicate that it belongs to a different tribe or even subfamily from *Elaphe*, but actually so little is known of the structure of all the other rat snakes that it still is too early to jump to conclusions. There seems little doubt that the Red-tail should be placed in its own genus, however.

THE BROWN GREENIE

Also placed in its own genus is the so-called Green Rat Snake, *Senticolis triaspis*, of Mexico and Central America, barely entering the United States in the mountains of the Arizona-New Mexico-Mexico border. This is a species that deserves a new common name, as it really is not a green snake over much of the range and even when green usually is just pale greenish tan or greenish yellow. The species is one of the most elongate rat snakes, with a long snout and head, protuberant eyes, and a long tail. Juveniles and sometimes adults have many (40 to over 70) short brown saddles over the back, these sometimes becoming obscure in adults. There are many scale rows around the body, usually over 33 and as many as 39 at midbody, more than in any other rat snakes. The most distinctive characters of the genus concern the hemipenis, which is not lobed and has gigantic thorns at the base. Perhaps the hemipenes could serve as a source of a new common name, the Thorny Rat Snake?

Though specimens from Arizona are pale greenish, as you go further south the snakes become more brownish overall and more strikingly patterned with brown blotches, at least south to the Yucatan area, then the brown blotches begin to be lost in the brown background, until snakes from Guatemala and Costa Rica are almost uniformly bright brown. Contrary to many previous reports, this species is most active during the cool of the morning and evening and is almost strictly a ground-dweller, seldom venturing higher than low shrubs. In nature it seems to feed (at least in southern Arizona) almost exclusively on deer mice and similar small mammals. Most specimens are between 3 and 5 feet long.

Keeping this snake is difficult or virtually impossible as it is very delicate, wild-caught specimens are heavily infected with a variety of

R. D. BARTLETT

A juvenile Green Rat Snake, *Senticolis triaspis mutabilis*, is far from green. Even when fully adult, most Green Rats are some shade of olive or tan.

parasites, and few specimens will take food regularly in the terrarium. For details, I suggest you read the article by T. Cranston in *The Vivarium*, 2(1): 8-11,23, Oct. 1989, to see what you will be up against if you try this species. This one is definitely for the advanced keeper. Enjoy trying to see one next time you are in the Chiricahua Mountains of southeastern Arizona or are vacationing in the Yucatan.

Though difficult for the beginner, the Trans-Pecos Rat Snake, *Bogertophis subocularis subocularis*, is one of the most gentle of the rat snakes. Few specimens live long in captivity, however.

R. D. BARTLETT

THE BROWNIES

Just to have a catchy common name, and to match the subjects of the previous section, I'm calling the two species of *Bogertophis* "brownies" because of their very distinctive tan or light brown coloration, especially on the unmarked head. Additionally, the species from the United States, *Bogertophis subocularis*, was described by Arthur E. Brown in 1901, making it one of the last full species of snakes discovered in the United States. It's time to give Brown his due!

BOGERT'S SNAKES

These are extremely distinctive snakes that do not seem to be closely related to more typical North American *Elaphe* and probably are derived from a different ancestor. In fact, the original describers of *Bogertophis* suggested that it is more closely related to the pine snakes than to the *Elaphe* rat snakes. The major technical characters for the genus lie mainly in the hemipenes of the male, features not readily noted by keepers, but the general appearance of the species is equally distinctive. The head is elongated, with a long snout and large, protuberant eyes. The neck is thin and very distinct from the head. With no known exception, there are no markings of any type on the top of the head, which is plain brown. The body is long and rather slim for a rat snake, and the pattern, if present, consists of darker brown markings on a brown to pale reddish brown background. Most distinctively, there is a row of three to seven scales under each eye and above the upper lip scales, the suboculars or lorilabials, unique among the North American rat snake group (and very

uncommon in Asian species) and easy to see in living specimens.

TRANS-PECOS RAT SNAKES

Currently two species of brownies are recognized, and one is fairly common in the hobby though it is far from an easy species to keep and breed. This species, the Trans-Pecos Rat Snake, *Bogertophis subocularis*, is found in the dry, rocky canyons and hillsides of western Texas, southern New Mexico, and northeastern Mexico. It bears a pair of distinctive narrow brown stripes on the otherwise unmarked neck, while the body bears numerous brown saddles. In the subspecies from Texas and New Mexico (*B. subocularis subocularis*), the saddles are H-shaped, very narrow in the center of the back and almost dash-like at the edges. Often the legs of the H are connected into a stripe on each side, especially on the front third of the body. The subspecies from Durango, Mexico (*B. subocularis amplinotus*) has the saddles much broader and more normal-looking, not as strongly pinched in at the center. The neck striping of the two subspecies also differs, being somewhat wavy (actually slightly wider spots connected by narrower stripes) in the Texas subspecies and very regular, without a wavy appearance, in the Durango subspecies.

In the lower Pecos River area of Texas the snakes become very pale sandy tan and the dorsal saddles become reduced in size and often assume very unusual shapes. This is the "blond" form of the species, a type that is bred in captivity with regularity and is preferred by many keepers. Though the Durango subspecies seems to be unknown in the hobby (it is a relatively plain snake by Trans-Pecos Rat Snake standards), obviously it has contributed genes to some of the captive-bred blond strains in the hobby because some of these snakes have wide saddles that do not resemble H's at all. Blond specimens often lack the neck stripes, by the way, and completely striped specimens have been bred as well.

The Trans-Pecos Rat Snake usually is some 4 to 5 feet long, big enough to hurt when it bites, but it has a reputation as one of the most gentle rat snakes, seldom biting. Its passive nature may be part of the reason many keepers have a problem keeping this snake, as it is nocturnal and often does not take food in captivity. It should be kept a bit warmer than typical, at least 81 to 90°F (27 to 32°C) in the substrate (just the warmer part of the terrarium, of course; remember the temperature gradient), with hotter basking areas. Remember that in nature rocks absorb heat during the day and stay warm well into the night, when these snakes are active.

This is a species that might benefit from the "black light" emitters that produce heat for basking with little or no visible light. It must be kept dry, like its natural habitat, but given drinking water as usual. Whether UV light is necessary for this species is controversial.

Present the food, especially pinkies, at dusk when the snake is most likely to find it. You may have to feed living food to these snakes, especially when you first get a Trans-Pecos. Remember to never leave mice that are mobile in the terrarium with a snake, however, or you will have a mouse-chewed pet the next day. It is possible that some of these snakes feed on lizards more often than small mammals, so you might want to try House Geckos or similar captive-bred lizards as food. Feed twice a week, more often if the snake is actively taking food, and consider yourself lucky if your pet feeds well.

Always buy only captive-bred Trans-Pecos Rat Snakes if you want to have any chance of keeping and breeding these snakes. Like their other activities, mating occurs at night, producing about six eggs that

If you have the urge to try to keep a Trans-Pecos Rat, *Bogertophis subocularis*, stick with captive-bred stock that is used to eating frozen and thawed mice. A mouse a week should be sufficient for most adult snakes.

R. D. BARTLETT

will hatch in three months or a bit less if incubated at 80 to 85°F (27 to 30°C) in a simple incubator with a vermiculite substrate. Sexual maturity is reached in three years.

BAJA RARITY

Bogertophis rosaliae, the Baja California Rat Snake, is very much like a slightly reddish brown, almost patternless version of the Trans-Pecos Rat Snake, sharing a similar shape, plain brown head, and row of lorilabials under the eye. Until very recently this was one of the most rarely collected North American snakes, and even today it is far from common. Apparently it has been bred in captivity a few times, but currently it is not available to the average hobbyist.

Found only in Baja California, Mexico (though there are persistent rumors that the species occurs in southern California), this is a species of dry, often nearly sterile canyons. It is nocturnal or at least not likely to be found in full sunlight, and feeds on the usual small mammals and birds and probably on lizards as well. The juvenile has a distinctive pattern of numerous narrow white bands about a scale wide over the middle of the back, these sometimes forming an irregular network. By a year or so of age these white bands are gone, leaving a plain pale reddish brown snake that reaches at least 3 feet in length in average specimens.

Though the coloration is very plain, to me this snake has a rather distinguished look, perhaps because the large eye is so well set-off from the head and provides the only spot of contrast in the color pattern. Unfortunately little has been published on keeping this snake, though it does like it warm and dry like the Trans-Pecos Rat Snake. Considering how difficult it sometimes is to keep a Trans-Pecos Rat, the Baja California Rat may be too difficult for beginners to keep even if it should become available.

The Baja California Rat Snake, *Bogertophis rosaliae*, is a species not likely to be seen in the pet shops for a few years.

R. D. BARTLETT

SUGGESTED READING

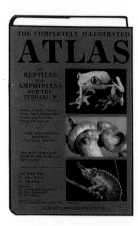

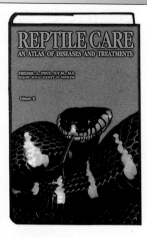

H-1102, 830 pgs, 1800+ photos

TS-165, TWO VOLUME SET, 655 pgs, 1850+ photos

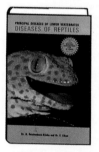

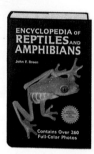

PS-207, 230 pgs, B&W Illus.

H-935, 576 pgs, 260+ photos

PS-876, 384 pgs, 175+ photos

KW-197, 128 pgs, 110+ photos

PB-126, 64 pgs, 32+ photos

AP-925, 160 pgs, 120+ photos

KW-197, 128 pgs, 110+ photos

J-007, 48 pgs, 25+ photos

TU-015, 64 pgs, 50+ photos

TW-111, 256 pgs, 180+ photos